eclipse
a journal

STEPHENIE MEYER

Megan Tingley Books

LITTLE, BROWN AND COMPANY

New York   Boston

Dear Reader,

You might have heard the story of how I started *Twilight*: I had a dream about the characters who would later become Bella and Edward. It was such a vivid and wonderful dream that I didn't want to forget it. And so I wrote and wrote, just for the sake of writing, just to see where the story would go.

I hope *The Twilight Journals* will encourage you to do the same. Filled with my favorite lines from the Twilight Saga and the works that inspired it, this journal is *your* space to write down your dreams, your memories, your stories, or anything you like.

I hope you enjoy your time writing as much as I have enjoyed mine.

I think it's something about the inevitability.
How nothing can keep them apart —
not her selfishness, or his evil, or even death, in the end. . . .
—Bella to Edward, on Wuthering Heights

Whatever our souls are made of, his and mine are the same;
and Linton's is as different as a moonbeam from lightning,
or frost from fire. — Cathy on Heathcliff, *Wuthering Heights*

If I had my way, I would spend the majority of my time kissing Edward. There wasn't anything I'd experienced in my life that compared to the feeling of his cool lips, marble hard but always so gentle, moving with mine. —Bella

Until now, there had never been a secret
I couldn't tell her. —Bella on Renée

It felt sort of like homesickness, this longing for the place and person who had sheltered me through my darkest night.
—Bella on Jacob

You are . . . well, not exactly the love of my life,
because I expect to love you for much longer than that.
The love of my existence. —Bella to Edward

My life was feeling a lot like a game of dice right now—
would the next roll come up snake eyes? —Bella

What did Leah think of Emily's scars,
now that she knew the truth behind them?
Did it seem like justice in her eyes? —Bella

I'm discovering that I can sympathize with Heathcliff in ways I didn't think possible before. —Edward to Bella

I didn't know how to do this. How to say goodbye to Charlie and Renée... to Jacob... to being human. I knew exactly what I wanted, but I was suddenly terrified of getting it. —Bella

I've already made my choice. —Bella to Rosalie

My love for Linton is like the foliage in the woods:
    time will change it, I'm well aware, as winter changes the trees.
    My love for Heathcliff resembles the eternal rocks beneath:
a source of little visible delight, but necessary. — Cathy, *Wuthering Heights*

So . . . it's not that you're afraid you won't . . . like me as much when I'm different—when I'm not soft and warm and I don't smell the same? You really do want to keep me, no matter how I turn out? —Bella to Edward

You. That's what I'm keeping. You'll always be my Bella, you'll just be a little more durable. —Edward

You don't get to be human again, Bella.
This is a once-in-a-lifetime shot. — Alice

I tried to imagine telling my parents that I was getting married this summer. Telling Angela and Ben and Mike. I couldn't. I couldn't think of the words to say.

It would be easier to tell them I was becoming a vampire. —Bella

I hoped that I would be as strong as Edward said I would be. Strong and fast and, most of all, beautiful. Someone who could stand next to Edward and feel like she belonged there. —Bella

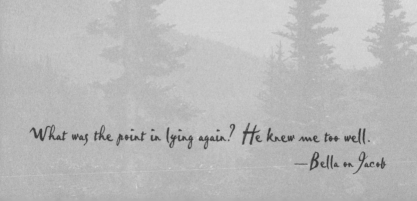

What was the point in lying again? He knew me too well.
—Bella on Jacob

All around us, my friends and neighbors and petty enemies ate and laughed and swayed to the music, oblivious to the fact that they were about to face horror, danger, maybe death. Because of me. —Bella

I wondered if I was a monster. . . the real kind.
The kind that hurt people. The kind that had no limits
when it came to what they wanted. —Bella

I was ready to join his family and his world. . . . He would never have to make the choice between me and his family again. We would be partners, like Alice and Jasper. Next time, I would do my part. —Bella on Edward

He was too beautiful. What was the word he'd used just now? Unbearable—that was it. His beauty was too much to bear. . . .

—Bella on Edward

I lived through an entire twenty-four hours thinking that you were dead, Bella. That changed the way I look at a lot of things. —Edward

Can you consider the idea that
 I might be better for her than you are?
                              —Jacob to Edward

You know, Jacob, if it weren't for the fact that we're natural enemies and that you're also trying to steal away the reason for my existence, I might actually like you. —Edward

You loved me—then what *right* had you to leave me?. . .
You, of your own will, did it. I have not broken your heart—
you have broken it; and in breaking it, you have broken mine.
—Heathcliff to Cathy, *Wuthering Heights*

I was selfish, I was hurtful. I tortured the ones I loved.
I was like Cathy, like Wuthering Heights, only my options were
so much better than hers, neither one evil, neither one weak.
And here I sat, crying about it, not doing anything productive
to make it right. Just like Cathy. —Bella

I couldn't allow what hurt me to influence my decisions anymore.
It was too little, much too late,
but I had to do what was right now. . . .
Edward would never see me shed another tear for Jacob Black.

—Bella

I had to get over this irrational feeling that Jacob belonged in my life. He couldn't belong with me, could not be my Jacob, when I belonged to someone else. —Bella

Despite all my intentions to cut Jacob out of my life completely, I didn't realize until that precise second exactly how deep the knife would have to go to do it. —Bella

I just beheaded and dismembered a sentient creature not twenty yards from you. That doesn't bother you? —Edward to Bella

There were people who deserved sympathy. I wasn't one of them.

—Bella

If the world was the sane place it was supposed to be, Jacob and I would have been together. And we would have been happy. He was my soul mate in that world — would have been my soul mate still if his claim had not been overshadowed by something stronger, something so strong that it could not exist in a rational world. —Bella

I used to think of you that way, you know. Like the sun.
My personal sun. You balanced out the clouds nicely for me.
—Bella to Jacob

The clouds I can handle.
    But I can't fight with an eclipse.
        —Jacob to Bella

In every cloud, in every tree—filling the air at night, and caught by glimpses in every object by day—I am surrounded with her image! . . . The entire world is a dreadful collection of memoranda that she did exist, and that I have lost her!   —Heathcliff on Cathy, *Wuthering Heights*

I'll always be waiting in the wings, Bella.
　　　　　　　　　　　　　　　—Jacob